KU-570-322

How Your Body Works

Althea

Illustrated by
Frances Cony

Happy Cat Books

Use your hand to turn over the page, and your eyes and brain to see how your body works...

We all have a skeleton like this inside our bodies. Our skeleton is a frame to hold our body in shape, without it we would be floppy.

The skeleton also protects important parts of our body. When you were born you had over 300 bones. As you grow some of these bones fuse together, so adults have about 200 bones. Where two bones meet it is called a joint.

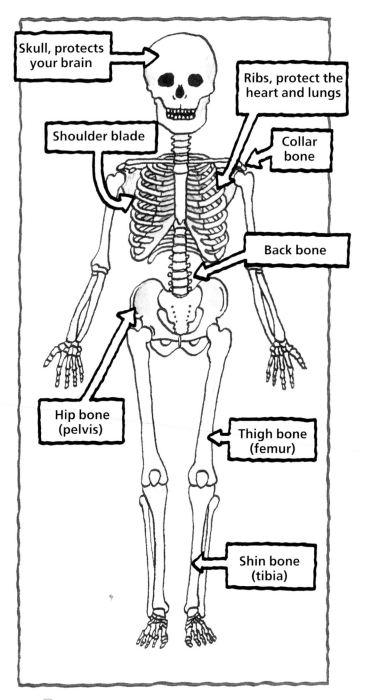

Skull, protects your brain

Ribs, protect the heart and lungs

Shoulder blade

Collar bone

Back bone

Hip bone (pelvis)

Thigh bone (femur)

Shin bone (tibia)

Some joints are hinged together like door hinges, making it possible to bend and stretch.

wiggle your finger

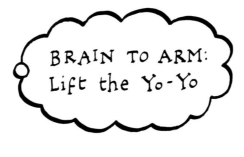

Your brain told your hand to wiggle your finger. Without your brain your body wouldn't work. To move your fingers, you also needed your muscles.

BRAIN TO ARM: Lift the Yo-Yo

Wires called nerves carry the messages from your brain to all parts of your body. When you want to lift your arm your brain sends messages to the muscles in your arm telling them to pull it up.

Muscles are attached to your bones by cords called tendons. You have more than 600 muscles which you use to move your joints and other parts of your body.

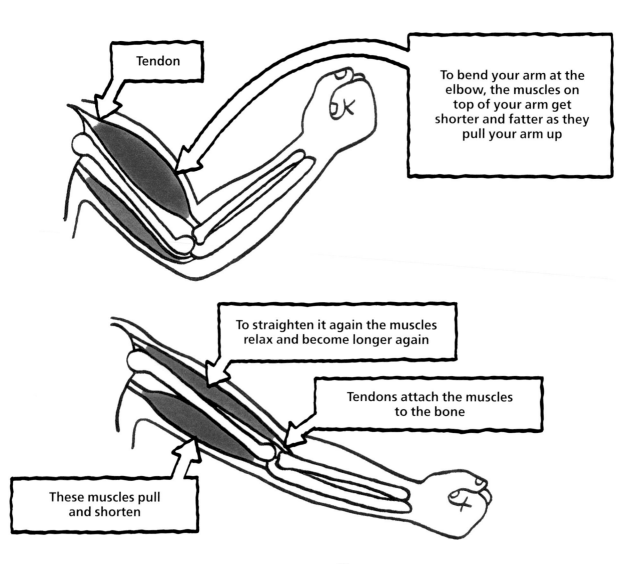

Tendon

To bend your arm at the elbow, the muscles on top of your arm get shorter and fatter as they pull your arm up

To straighten it again the muscles relax and become longer again

Tendons attach the muscles to the bone

These muscles pull and shorten

Can you wiggle your ears?

You may have to think very hard to use the right muscles to make you ears move.

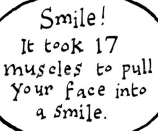

Smile!
It took 17
muscles to pull
your face into
a smile.

You have a strong muscle on either side of your mouth to pull your teeth together when you want to bite into food.

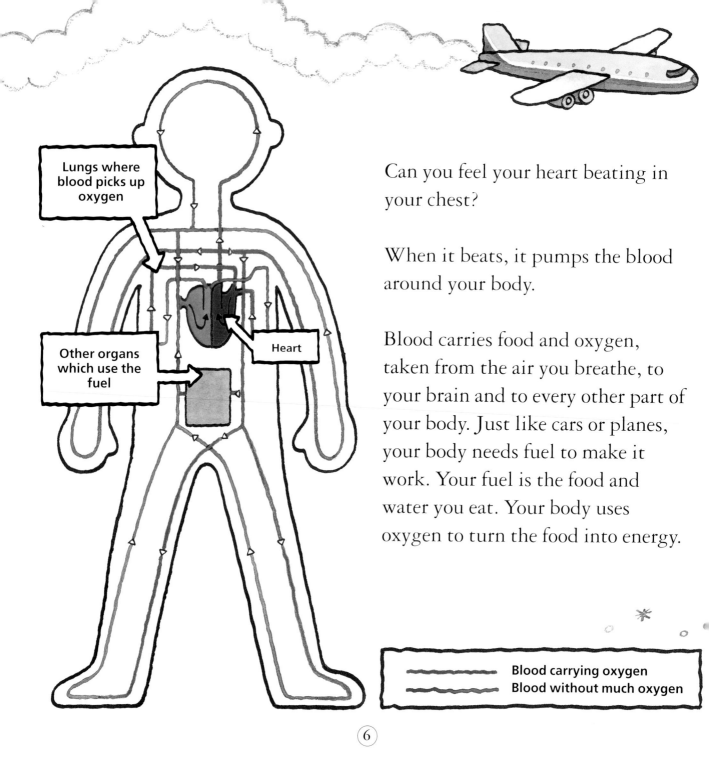

Lungs where blood picks up oxygen

Other organs which use the fuel

Heart

Can you feel your heart beating in your chest?

When it beats, it pumps the blood around your body.

Blood carries food and oxygen, taken from the air you breathe, to your brain and to every other part of your body. Just like cars or planes, your body needs fuel to make it work. Your fuel is the food and water you eat. Your body uses oxygen to turn the food into energy.

Blood carrying oxygen
Blood without much oxygen

Your heart beats about seventy
to ninety times a minute.
It beats faster if you are excited
or running about because you
are using more energy.

The air you breathe goes down your windpipe into your lungs. The blood pumping around your body takes oxygen from this air. You then breathe out the waste gases.

As soon as you were born you started to breathe.

Windpipe

Air (filtered by hairs and sticky stuff)

Waste gas (made in your body)

Lung   Lung

Have you... noticed... that you... need to breathe... more often... when you... are running..?

Woof ...Woof

You need extra oxygen because you need more energy.

Do you breathe through your mouth? Or your nose?

It's better to use your nose, because the sticky stuff and hairs in your nose stop germs and dirt from getting into your lungs. Your lungs have more sticky stuff which is coughed up when it gets dirty.

Dirt or dust may make us sneeze.
The sneeze blows dust or germs out of your nose.
Try and use a hanky!

Aah choo

- Bitter
- Sour
- Salt
- Sweet

Tiny bumps on your tongue, called taste buds, recognise different tastes. If something tastes very bitter or sour, it may be a warning that it's not good for you.

When you eat, your teeth chew food small to make it easier to swallow. Your tongue mixes the food with the spit, called saliva, in your mouth. When you are ready to swallow, the food is pushed down the tube called the oesophagus to your stomach.

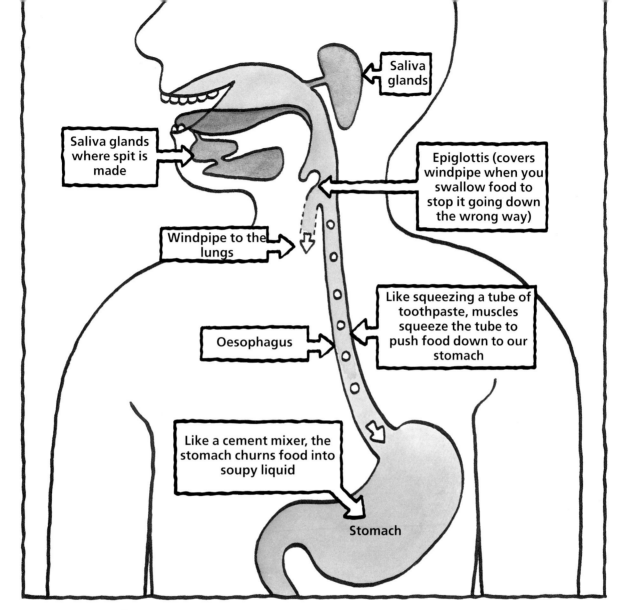

Food must be turned into liquid before it can get into your blood. Your stomach mixes digestive juices with the food and after about four hours it changes into a thick soup.

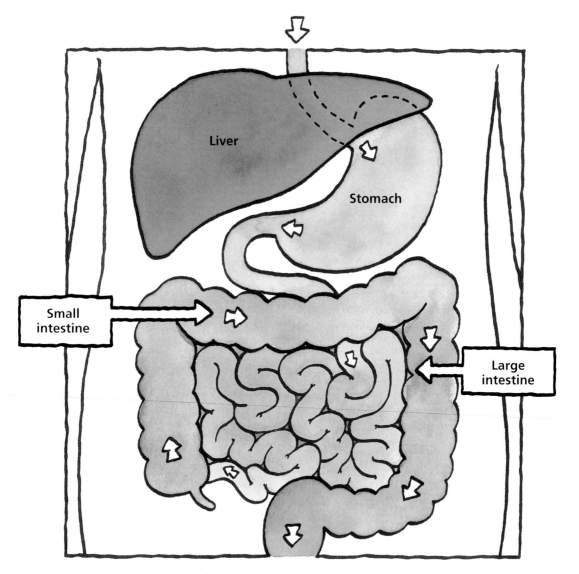

The soupy liquid then travels into a long wiggly tube called the small intestine. More juices are added, and the liquid becomes thinner. This digested food can pass through the walls of the tube into your blood.

You need water in every part of your body. Water comes from food as well as drink. Some water is used to make blood. Each time your blood is pumped round your body it passes through the kidneys to be cleaned.

About 60% of our body is made of water.

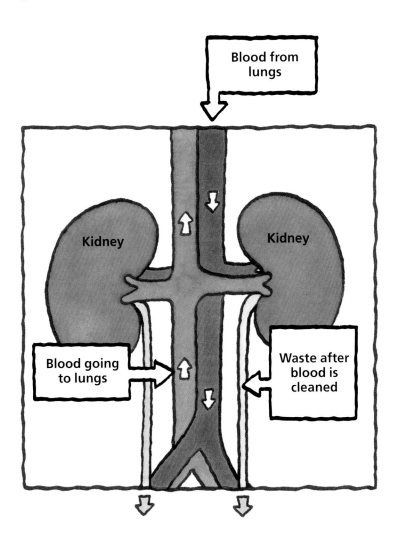

Water carries the waste from your kidneys to your bladder. You know when your bladder is full because you need to go to the toilet.

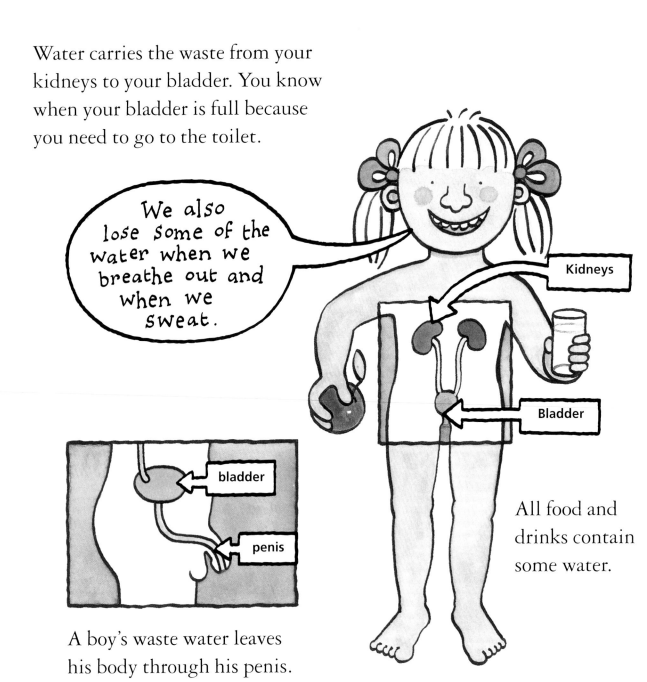

We also lose some of the water when we breathe out and when we sweat.

Kidneys

Bladder

bladder

penis

All food and drinks contain some water.

A boy's waste water leaves his body through his penis.

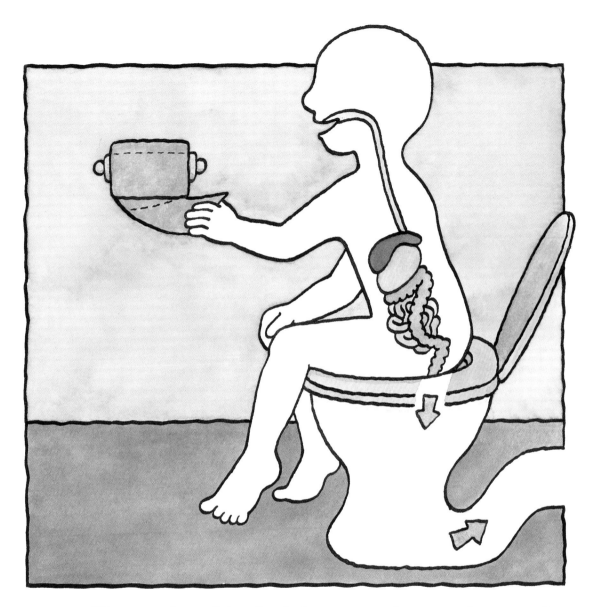

The remains of the food that cannot be turned
into liquid passes along the large intestine to
your bottom, ready to go down the toilet.

Skin is stretchy and covers all the outside of your body. It stops dirt and germs from getting into your body. Skin also protects you from sun and rain. The darker the colour of your skin, the more it protects you from the sun. Your skin is waterproof, so you don't get soggy when you have a bath or are out in the rain. It has very tiny holes in it, to let you sweat when it's very hot. As the sweat dries it cools your skin.

Where did I put those scissors?

You are making new skin cells all the time. The old dead skin cells fall off. When you graze or cut yourself, the dried blood makes a scab to protect you, while the new skin grows underneath.

Nails protect the tops of your fingers. Hair and nails grow and need cutting – they don't fall off by themselves!

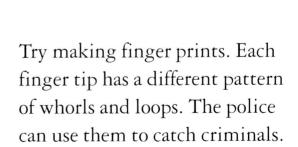

Try making finger prints. Each finger tip has a different pattern of whorls and loops. The police can use them to catch criminals.

Your brain and your nervous system control your body. It makes you breathe in and out and keeps your heart beating, even when you are asleep. It also tries to make sense of the world around you.

You see with your eyes

You smell with your nose

You taste with your tongue

You hear with your ears

You touch with your fingers and the rest of your skin

You feel all over

Your eyes, ears, nose, tongue, skin and other parts of your body, collect information and send messages along your nerve cells to your brain.

Your eyes move up and down and from side to side, so you can see what is going on around you – but not behind you.

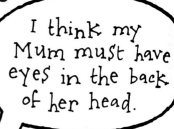

I think my Mum must have eyes in the back of her head.

Your eyelids keep blinking to wash liquid over your eyes, to protect them and keep them clean.

When you cry, tears trickle down your cheeks. This is because the drain in the corner of your eyes isn't big enough to take away all the extra liquid made in the tear ducts.

Some people need glasses to help them see things clearly. . .

cle arly.

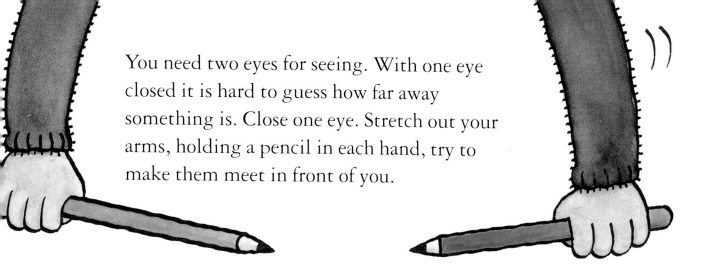

You need two eyes for seeing. With one eye closed it is hard to guess how far away something is. Close one eye. Stretch out your arms, holding a pencil in each hand, try to make them meet in front of you.

Without your brain, you wouldn't know what you are looking at. Sometimes it may be difficult for your brain to work out what it is seeing. What can you see, a pretty girl or an old woman? If you keep staring at the picture you will see both.

Can your brain understand this fork?

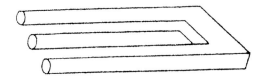

Your nose and your tongue collect smells and tastes and pass this information to your brain.

As well as enjoying nice tastes and smells (like ice cream), your brain warns you of danger, like the smell of burning.

You can make different noises as you breathe out. By changing the shape of your lips, and using your teeth and tongue you make words and sounds.

Your ears collect sounds and send them to your brain. It will work out what they mean and what you should do.

Often our brain works so quickly that we don't realise it is having to work. We may answer without knowing we had to think about it.

The inner ear is filled with liquid. The liquid stays level when you move, like carrying a bottle of water. It helps you keep your balance.

Spin round and round, and then stop. Are you dizzy? That's because the liquid is still spinning in your ears.

When you started to understand language your brain stored words and their meanings in your memory. Some people are better at remembering things than others. This is how we learn to understand one another. Sometimes this can be very difficult.

You are learning new things all the time.

Perhaps you have learnt something new from this book?

As you learn new things the information is stored in your brain so you can use it at a later date. In the same way computers store information, but computers can't think.

Brains have to make sense of the information they are sent. When you think, that is what your brain is doing. Brains are all different from each other. So are people.

Sometimes your brain makes pictures to try and help you understand your thoughts and feelings.

When you are laughing and happy or sad and feeling like crying, or frightened, or angry, or excited, it is our brain which tries to sort out all these feelings.

When you are asleep your brain makes more pictures and stories. Sometimes you can remember these dreams when you wake up. Some dreams are very strange. If you are having a bad dream you may be able to tell yourself to wake up.

There are lots of things you can do to help keep your body healthy.

Running about and playing games keeps your bones and muscles in good repair.

You also need to rest and to sleep.

Baths and showers wash the dirt from your skin and hair.

Always wash your hands after going to the toilet and before a meal, in case you lick your fingers and let germs in through your mouth.

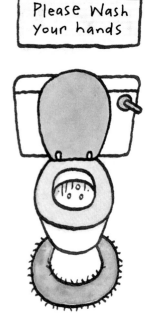

Please Wash Your hands

When the sun is very bright you may need to wear a hat and cream to protect your skin from burning.

Having three meals a day and eating lots of fruit and vegetables keep you healthy and full of energy.

Don't forget to clean your teeth.

Never eat a berry off a bush or a sweet unless an adult you know tells you it is all right. Some medicines, called drugs, look like sweets, but they can make you very ill.

Index